Prayer Thoughts for
High School Boys

Lord,
I've Been
Thinking

RON KLUG

AUGSBURG Publishing House • Minneapolis

Contents

To Lyn
for her encouragement and help

A word about prayer

"It was the best of times. It was the worst of times." Charles Dickens said that about the French Revolution. But his words also describe the teenage years. They can be the best of times—as you grow physically, emotionally, spiritually; as you make new friends, achieve independence, experience fun and excitement. But they can also be the worst of times—filled with self-doubt, problems, worries, and temptations.

Most of us need all the help we can get to make it through the teenage years successfully—help from friends, parents, pastors, counselors, and most of all from God.

One of the ways God helps us is through prayer. When we pray, we come consciously into God's presence and open our lives to him. And he responds by giving us forgiveness, strength, courage, and guidance. We pray for others too, and in this way we cooperate with God, releasing his power into the lives of those who need him.

In one sense, prayer is our natural response to God, but in another sense we must learn to pray, and in the school of prayer we never graduate. We always have more to learn.

When you were a child, you may have learned to memorize and recite certain prayers, but now as you grow spiritually, you can learn to speak to God in your own words, about all phases of your life. At first this may be hard to do. One of the purposes of this book is to help you identify your feelings and problems and find words to express them.

The prayers concern each of the four major relationships in your life: your relationship to yourself, your relationship to others, your relationship to the world, and your relationship to God. A balanced prayer life includes prayers about each of these relationships.

Not every prayer in this book will fit you or your life. Some may express very well how you feel. Others you can change to fit your situation—or just ignore them. Best of all, you can use these prayers as a springboard to create your own prayers—on paper, if you like to write; out loud; or just in your mind.

Written prayers like these are also useful during times when we experience "spiritual dryness," when we feel too tired or when it seems impossible to pray. Then written prayers can help us over the slump until spiritual freshness returns.

My prayer is that as you use this book, you will be helped to come before God in total honesty, admitting all your feelings and problems and expressing them to him. I know he will hear you, and answer. He may not answer immediately. And he may not answer exactly the way you expect. But his answer will be what you really need at that time.

My real feelings

Why is it so hard for me to tell others
what I really think
or how I really feel?
I care so much about what people think of me,
and I hate to look foolish.
I don't want people to laugh at me.
So sometimes I don't say anything,
or I just make a joke
or say something dumb.
Sometimes I can't even admit to *myself*
that I feel a certain way
or that I think certain thoughts.
And so I go through life wearing a mask.

I don't like being frightened and self-conscious.
I'd like to be able to tell people
my real feelings and ideas
without being so afraid of what they'll think.
Lord, help me sometimes to risk,
to express my real feelings,
even though others may laugh.
It's better to be laughed at
than to be an unreal shadow.

Lord, I'm glad that I can tell you
all that I am and feel and think.
Give me courage to be open with
others too.

Decisions, decisions

Lord, every day I have to make choices
between what's right and what's wrong,
and lots of times I don't know how to choose.
Sometimes the decisions are clear-cut,
spelled out in your Word
or in the law
or in family or school rules.
But other decisions aren't so obvious.
Our world today is so complicated,
and we have so many options.
There isn't just one set of answers
or even one set of questions.

Help me know how to make good decisions
using the wisdom of the past,
the advice of family and friends,
and my own best thoughts.
Forgive me when I make wrong choices.
Help me learn from my mistakes.
Keep on guiding me by your Spirit.
And as I see what is right in each new situation,
give me the courage and strength to do it.

So self-conscious

I have to give a speech in class,
and I dread it.
When I know I'm going to have to get up
in front of everyone,
I'm nervous for days.
I feel so uncomfortable in front of a group.
Why am I so self-conscious, Lord?
I hate it.
I can feel myself turning red,
and I fidget around.
I know if I make a mistake
everyone will laugh,
and I hate to look foolish.
I want to be self-confident,
cool,
competent,
self-assured.

O God, be with me
when I have to get up in front of the class
or walk into a room full of people
or be introduced to strangers.
Help me overcome my fears and self-consciousness.
Give me the confidence that comes from knowing
that you are with me
and that I don't look foolish to you.

Who am I?

"Learn to be yourself," someone said to me.
But what self should I be?
I don't even know who I am.
Sometimes I feel like a chameleon:
I change colors to match my surroundings.
When I'm with one bunch of friends I act one way.
When I'm with others I act totally different.
I try to be whatever they want me to be.
Some days I feel like half a dozen people.
One minute I'm The Good Student,
Then I'm The Great Hero,
then The Bold Lover,
then The Tough Fighter,
then The Great Comedian,
then The Pious Christian.
Which is the real me?

Lord, you must know who I am.
You made me and you know all my thoughts.
Help me see myself as you see me.
Then I'll begin to learn who I really am.

No self-discipline

I just don't have very much self-discipline.
I make good resolutions and promises,
but I don't keep them.
It's really hard for me to make myself practice
or do homework
when I don't feel like it.
I'd rather do what I feel like doing.
But then I waste time and get behind in everything.

Other people seem to be so well-organized.
They *always* get things done on time.
They work hard at something,
and then they are really good at it.
They must have more willpower than I do.

Lord, help me learn self-discipline.
Help me work at long-term goals
and not just act on my spur-of-the-moment feelings.
Show me how to make the best use of my time
and how to follow through on my good resolutions.

A different drummer

I like the words of Thoreau:
"If a man does not keep pace with his companions,
perhaps it is because he hears a different drummer."
I want to be like that,
listening to my own drummer
and not just following the crowd.

But sometimes it's really hard.
The voice of the crowd is loud and persistent,
and sometimes I can't hear my drummer.
The crowd has a way of cutting down people
who are different.
I'm afraid of being laughed at or rejected.
I want to be an individual,
but I don't want people to think I'm strange.
And I don't want to be a nonconformist
just for the sake of being different.

Lord, help me understand when nonconformity
is right for me.
Help me hear my own drummer
and keep my own pace.

Send me some friends

I wish I had more friends,
some good ones I could count on.
I know a lot of kids,
but hardly any are my close friends.
Either I don't like them
or they don't like me
or we're too different from one another.
I wish I had some friends
who like to do what I like,
talk about what interests me,
go places I like to go.
But it's hard to find people like that.

Is there something wrong with me?
Is there something that I'm not doing that I should?
Show me how to be a good friend, Lord.
Teach me about friendship
and send me some good friends.

A faith of my own

Lord, when I was just a baby,
my parents brought me to you.
All the while I was a child
they took me to church and Sunday school
and saw to it that I said my prayers.
All this happened whether I wanted it or not.
I had no choices.

But now I'm old enough to choose for myself.
I want my faith to be my own,
not just something I inherited.
I have to figure things out for myself.
Thank you for parents, pastors, teachers, and friends
who helped me this far along the way.
I know you were at work in my life through them.
Accept me now on my own.
Continue to give me the people
and books
and experiences I need
to keep me moving forward
in my life with you.

Trying to look good

Lord, I'm tired of trying to look good all the time
so the other kids will like me.
I'm tired of always trying to look smart
and competent
and strong
and in control.
It's hard to remember
to say the right thing,
laugh at the right time,
wear the right clothes,
watch the right TV shows,
go to the right movies,
be seen with the right kids.

Sometimes I feel like I have to do all that
so I can be popular.
But I'm tired of playing that game.
Lord, don't let me care so much about popularity
that I lose my own self.
Give me good friends, Lord,
who will like me
even when I make mistakes,
friends who will like me for myself.

My first job

I have my first job!
I'm glad I can start making some money on my own.
That will help my parents,
and I can buy some things I need and want.
I like feeling independent.

Help me to do this job,
to serve my employer well,
and to serve you through my work.

Bless everyone who works at useful jobs,
especially those whose work is boring
or dangerous
or beyond their powers.
And help those who would like to work but can't
because of sickness of body or mind,
or lack of skills or education,
or because of a shortage of jobs.

Thanks for my job, Lord.
Help me do it well.

Be real for me

Lord, some of my friends seem to know you so well.
They talk about you as their best friend
and tell me they're sure they have Jesus in their heart.
They seem to see you involved
in every little detail of their lives.
I wonder if that's really true for them,
or if they've just been taught
certain words and phrases.
If it is true,
I'd like to have faith like theirs.
I'd like to know you as well
as they claim to.
But sometimes you seem so far away,
and I don't want to *pretend* you're near
just so I can sound like my friends.

I'd like a close relationship with you, Lord.
Be real for me.

I'm not dating yet

Lord, lots of my friends are dating
and have regular girl friends.
I don't have a girl friend
and I don't really want one.
I wonder why I'm so slow to grow up.
I don't feel ready for dating.

When I am ready,
I wonder whether there will be
someone who wants to go out with me.
Will the girl I like
like me too?
Will dating be fun,
or will it be a big hassle?

Lord, stick by me.
Help me remember that I don't have to follow
someone else's pattern.
Let me be satisfied with growing up at my own pace.

My friend died

My friend died, Lord.
Before, death always seemed far away,
something that happened to old people
or people I didn't know.
Now for the first time
I feel it close by.

I wonder why he had to die.
He was a good person.
He could have done a lot of good in the world.
Why, Lord?
I'll miss him.
And his family will miss him.
I hope this isn't the end for him,
that he's alive with you.
Help me remember that Jesus rose from the dead
so all who believe in him
will live forever with you.

Lord, I know I could die too.
I wonder if I would be ready.
Make me ready to face death—
my friend's death
and my own—
knowing that death isn't the end for us,
that beyond death we will always be with you.

Make us care

It seems that people are fighting all over the world.
So many things divide people:
language,
color,
age,
education,
money,
customs,
politics,
even religion.

Yet we're all your children.
Lord, take away the barriers that keep people apart
and that make people fight one another.
Help us move toward the dream of Jesus:
"That they may be one."
Bless the people who are working
in all parts of the world
to bring understanding and peace and love.

Help me in my world—
at home
at school
at church
in the neighborhood—
to be a peacemaker,
bringing people together.

I like cars

I can't wait to get my driver's license.
I like cars
and anything that has a motor in it.
When I was small, I always enjoyed
bikes and toy trucks and cars.
Now I'm eager to get behind the wheel of the real thing.
Lord, help me remember that a car isn't a toy.
It's a powerful machine that can kill and destroy.
I want the freedom to go on my own
without being dependent on my parents,
but help me remember that with that freedom
goes responsibility.
When I'm tempted to show off
or take chances,
give me a cool head.
Help me drive safely.

Protect me when I drive
and protect those with me.
Help me be alert and careful.
I want to be a good driver.

So many words

Why do we have to use so many words in church?
Sometimes religion just seems to be
words, words, words.
I hear the pastor say *salvation, grace, redemption,*
sin, forgiveness, sanctification,
and they're just words.
They don't make anything happen inside me.
I've heard some of them so many times
they seem empty.
During the sermon
my mind wanders to the ball game
that afternoon.
I sing through a whole hymn
and realize I haven't paid attention
to any of the words.
Lord, I want words to have meaning
and not be empty.
Let your spirit make the words come alive.
May the words I hear in church
and the words of my prayers
have real meaning for my life.

I'm sick

I'm sick, Lord, and I don't like it.
I don't want to be in bed,
away from my friends,
unable to do all the things I like to do.
I want to get well.

Even so, this time isn't all bad.
I like the break from school.
It's a good time to relax,
do some thinking,
read a good book,
talk with you.
Lord, let this be a good time for me.

Bless those who care for me now.
Bless all the forces at work
to bring healing in my body.
Give me health and energy again.
Lord, I thank you
that your healing power is at work in my body,
that you are healing me now.

Sex is powerful

Sex is powerful and mysterious.
It seems to have a power all its own,
strong enough to overcome
willpower and good sense,
and make people mess up their lives.
Sex is fascinating.
I like to talk about it with friends.
It's exciting in a way no other subject is.
But it's scary too.
I know something about sex
from parents, friends, and teachers.
But I don't always know what's true.
And I'm too embarrassed to ask anyone.

Help me understand about sex, Lord,
and give me a good attitude about it.
Help me remember it's not something
dirty or shameful or funny,
but that it is one of your gifts.
Because this gift is so powerful,
you've set boundaries around it
so we don't use it to hurt ourselves or other people.
Help me to know what the boundaries are for me
at this time in my life.
Help me enjoy this powerful gift
within the boundaries you've set.

People of all races

When I read about the days of slavery in our country,
I can hardly believe it.
How could people be so cruel to other people
just because they were a different color?

I know the problem isn't just in the past.
Racism is still with us
in this country
and in other parts of the world.
People are still mistreated because they're black
or red
or yellow
or white.
Lord, why does skin color
make so much difference to us?

Help me, first of all,
to recognize my own racism and prejudice
and to overcome it.
Show me what I can do to help people of all colors
live together in peace,
right now,
right where I am.
And help me to love the racists.
They need our understanding too.
Forgive us for our prejudice
and bring a new day of peace.

I wish I had some privacy

I wish I had some privacy,
some space and time I could call my own,
a place that was mine
where no one else could come in.
I'm tired of having no place
where I can be alone.

It's more than just having a room of my own.
I wish I didn't always have to say
where I've been
and who I was with
and what I did.
Why can't my parents just trust me?

Help me see my parents' side,
and help them realize I need some privacy.

Money, money, money

Lord, sometimes I think I'd like to have a lot of money,
to buy the things I want,
to travel,
to give to those who need it.
Sometimes I think about money a lot.

Teach me to have a good perspective about money
and what it can buy.
Help me be thankful to you for the money I have
and for the good things I can buy with it.
Help me spend my money wisely,
so I don't waste it on things with no lasting value.
Keep me from selfishness.
Help me remember those who have less than I do,
and make me willing to share with those who are poor
in this country
and throughout the world.
Let money be a gift I use for your purposes.

Help me pass the test

Lord, a big test is coming up,
and I'm nervous.
I need to get a good grade,
and I'm afraid I'll fail.
Then my parents will really be on me.
And when the tests are handed back,
everyone will be asking
"What did you get?"
and I don't want to look dumb.

Sometimes I study hard for a test
and think I'm really ready.
Then the day comes and I sit at my desk
with a sick feeling in my stomach.
The teacher hands out the test,
I look at it—
and my mind goes blank.
I can't remember anything,
and I do a rotten job.
Then the teacher makes some remark like
"Maybe a little studying would help."

I'm afraid that will happen again.
O God, be with me when I take this test.
Help me to think clearly
and to remember what I've learned.
Help me pass the test, Lord.

Where is the Spirit?

Lots of people in the church
are talking about the Holy Spirit—
and I'm confused.
Does the Holy Spirit
have to do with Baptism and Communion,
worship and the Bible?
Or with speaking in tongues,
miracles, healing, and emotional experiences?
Or is it both?
Does the Holy Spirit work in slow, quiet ways?
Or in strange and dramatic happenings?
Or is it both?
Is there something wrong with me if I don't have those
strange and dramatic experiences?
Are they something I should be seeking?

Help me understand what the Holy Spirit is
and how the Spirit works.
Let your Spirit work in my life, Lord,
in all sorts of ways,
in ways you know are right for me.
Keep me growing and moving
closer to you and your will.

I'm angry

Why am I angry so often?
I get mad at myself,
at my parents,
at brothers and sisters,
at teachers,
at other kids.
Sometimes I seem mad at the whole world.
Sometimes I even feel mad at you, God.

Is it wrong for me to feel so angry?
It seems like I can't help feeling this way.
But what do I do with my anger?
If I express it the wrong way, I may hurt people.
If I bury it in myself, it might poison me.
Help me know how I should handle my anger, Lord,
when to control it
and how to release it or express it
in ways that won't hurt others.

Love everyone?

I know we're supposed to love everyone,
but some people are really hard to love.
Right now there's one person
I just can't stand.
He's sloppy and dirty.
He's a big loudmouth.
He's always fighting and arguing.
He's sarcastic
and he tries to hurt people by the things he says.
He acts so weird,
I can't figure him out.
How can I begin to love him?

I suppose he needs a friend.
But I don't know how to be a friend to him.
And I'm afraid of what other kids will think of me
if I act like his friend.
I think he needs more help than I can give.

Send him help, Lord.
Let him know you love him.
Help me be good to him as much as I can,
and forgive me when my love falls short.
Thanks, Lord,
that your love is so much bigger than mine.

This body of mine

Sometimes I wish I didn't have a body—
at least not this one.
I feel clumsy and self-conscious.
I feel too big or too small
or too fat or too thin
or too *something*.
I look at others, and I wish I had
someone else's looks or build
or complexion or coordination.
Sometimes feelings come over me that I can't control,
and I do something that leaves me
feeling guilty and ashamed.
Or my body feels tired and dull
and all I want to do is lie around.
Then I wonder whether life would be better
if we didn't have bodies.

Other times I'm really glad I have a body.
I feel good when I run around the track
or connect with a solid hit
or sink a jump shot.
Sometimes I look in the mirror
and I like what I see.
I think, *You know, I don't look too bad.*
Sometimes I like this body of mine.

You made us with bodies, Lord,
and you must have had a good reason.
Help me live with this body of mine.
Help me take good care of it
so it will be a healthy body,
ready to serve you and other people.

I have so many questions

O God, how can I be sure you exist?
Some people seem so sure of what they believe,
and sometimes I am too,
but sometimes I just don't know.
I can't see you or hear you,
and I can't always feel your presence.
People tell me to believe the Bible,
but how can I know for sure the Bible is true?

I have so many questions, Lord.
I wish I had some answers.
I'm afraid to ask some of my questions,
afraid people will think I'm a doubter or an unbeliever.
Sometimes I pretend to believe everything
and give all the right answers
because I want people to think I'm a good Christian.
But inside, I'm not very sure.

Lord, help me understand
and help me believe.
Answer my doubts and questions.
If you're really there,
let me know you.
I want to be sure that you're real
and that you care about me.

Booze, pills, and grass

Some of my friends are experimenting
with drugs and alcohol.
They claim it gives them a high
and makes them feel good.
They say it's really fun.

Most of the time I think they're stupid
for messing around
with booze and pills and grass.
But sometimes I wonder what it would be like.
My friends seem to have such good times.
And I don't want them to think I'm afraid.
But I know drugs and alcohol can be dangerous.
They can damage a person's body and mind,
and they can be habit-forming.
My friends think this could never happen to them,
that they could never become alcoholics or junkies.
But I'm not so sure.

Lord, I really want to stay away from that stuff now,
no matter what my friends say.
Help me make wise decisions
about the use of drugs and alcohol.

Hard to please

O God, why are my parents so hard to please?
It seems like no matter how hard I try
it's never good enough for them.
Whenever I do something,
I know that as soon as I'm finished
they'll tell me what I did wrong.
If I get straight A's,
they'll complain because they weren't A plusses.
It seems like I just can't win.

I think they mean well.
They want me to be successful.
But they don't seem to understand
that I need some compliments once in a while.
I can't always be perfect.
I wish just once they would say
"You did a good job"
and not point out every place that needs improving.

Help my parents understand
that sometimes I need to feel good about myself.
Help me live with the pressure, Lord.
I know you love me,
even when I'm not perfect.

Thanks for books

Thanks for good books, Lord.
I can't imagine my life without them.
They bring me adventure,
mystery,
new ideas,
and new understandings.
Through books I meet people
I could never know any other way.
I like to escape into a good book
and lose myself in another world.
Good stories fill the hours
that would otherwise be boring or wasted.

Lord, keep providing us with good books.
Bless those who write
and edit
and illustrate
and sell
good books.
Help me make wise choices in what I read.

Rules, rules, rules

God, I'm so tired of rules.
I feel like my whole life is fenced in.
I'm suffocating under rules.
Do this.
Don't do that.
Keep off the grass.
No smoking.
No shirt no shoes no service.
Don't eat so fast.
Slow down.
Hurry up.
Be quiet.
Speak up.
Stop.

At school, at home, at church,
everywhere I go
I'm hemmed in by rules.
Sometimes I wish I could smash all the rules
and break out.
I know there have to be some rules
so people can live together,
but why do there have to be so many?

Lord, don't let me be so angry about the rules
that I do something stupid.
Help me live with the rules
and give me ways to be free.

Forgive me

Lord, I do so many things I know are wrong.
I hurt people with unkind words,
or suddenly I hear myself
saying something really crude or dirty.
Sometimes I'm impatient with my family and friends.
I get into arguments and fights
because I can't keep my mouth shut.
I don't always make the best use of my time.
I don't always do the work I should.
Often I want what I want, when I want it,
instead of thinking of others.
I forget to pray.
I don't love you, God, as I should.

Lord, when I look at this list, I feel discouraged.
I fall so far short of what you want me to be
and of what I want to be.
Forgive me, Lord.
Help me believe that you keep on loving me,
even when I fall so far short of your plans for me.
Help me learn from my mistakes.

Thank you for Jesus, who lived and died and rose
to free me from the power of sin,
whose life is a model for me to follow.
Even when I can't see anything but my faults,
I want to thank you for your Holy Spirit,
who is always working in my life,
making me more and more like Jesus.

Thanks for laughter

I like to laugh, Lord.
Sometimes I laugh so hard
I can't stop.
It feels so good to laugh.
Thanks, Lord, for people who are funny,
for good jokes,
for funny books and TV shows and movies.
Thanks for good laughter, Lord.

There's a kind of laughter that's not so good—
the sneering laugh that mocks someone
or puts people down,
the laugh that's used to embarrass others
or make them feel bad.
I don't like that kind of laughter
when it's used against me.
Sometimes I use laughter that way,
to hurt or embarrass someone,
but I don't feel good afterwards.

Keep me from using laughter as a weapon, Lord.
Send me lots of good times for laughing.
Let my laughter be clean and bright,
the kind that brings friendship and joy.

Who is this Jesus?

Sometimes I wonder who Jesus really is.
People have such different ideas about him.
Is he . . .
(a) a great man
(b) Son of God
(c) a fake
(d) a wise teacher
(e) none of the above?
How can I be sure which is right?

Sometimes Jesus seems very real to me,
and I can call him Lord,
Savior,
Friend.
Other times he seems like a great stranger,
and I wonder what he has to do with me.

God, help me know who Jesus is
and what he means for me.

We're moving

Lord, we're moving,
and my feelings about it are all mixed up.
I don't like leaving good friends behind,
going away from what I know and like.
Saying goodbye is going to be hard.
And I don't know much about the new place.
Will I like it?
Will I be able to find friends?
Will the school be OK?
It's not easy to be the new kid who moves in
when everybody else already has friends.
I'll probably feel awkward and self-conscious,
having to meet a whole bunch of new people.
Moving is scary.

But there's a good side too.
Not everything is perfect here.
There are some things and some people
I'll be glad to leave behind.
I look forward to a new place
and new experiences
and new people.

One thing I do know, Lord,
is that you'll move with us.
Wherever we go, you're there,
the same as always,
with your protection
and strength
and love.
Be with us as we move, Lord.

I wish I were older

Lord, I wish I were older.
I look at the older kids
and they seem so much more mature,
more self-confident,
not awkward and self-conscious like me.
They can do so many things I can't do.
They're more independent.
They seem happier,
less afraid.
I wish I were older.

Some people think that being a teenager is easy,
but I wish I were done with being a teenager.

I guess that's a useless wish.
I just can't skip my teenage years.
Help me make the most of this time of my life.
Help me be patient with my growing.

So many churches

There are so many churches,
so many religions.
How can I know which one is right?
Each one has its own holy book,
its own ways of worshiping,
different ways of talking,
different customs and rules.
How can I sort them all out?

Some people think
it doesn't make any difference what you believe.
Some think all religions are the same.
And others are sure theirs is the only right one.
How can I know?

Lord, I want to know the truth.
Show me who you are
and how I can know you.
Show me what's true
and what isn't.
Help me make some sense of this, O God.

Nobody understands me

Nobody understands me—
not my parents,
not my teachers,
not even my friends.
They don't really know who I am
or what I think about,
worry about,
dream about.
And I'm afraid to tell them
because they wouldn't understand.
They'd think something was wrong with me.

Some things I can talk about with my friends,
because I know they feel the way I do.
But some things I'm afraid to share even with them.
They might laugh
or think I'm different.

Lord, do you understand me?
I hope so, because you're my only hope.
Help me be honest with you.
Help me believe that you care for me
and that you understand.

Words are powerful

Little kids sometimes say,
"Sticks and stones may break my bones,
but words can never harm me."
But I know better.
Words can hurt a lot more than sticks and stones.
Words can be powerful weapons
to hurt people,
to embarrass them,
to make them feel small and insignificant.
Words like "ugly" or "stupid"
or "nigger" or "kook" or "mental"
can smash and cut
and leave someone bleeding on the inside.
Or words can be used to ridicule
what other people value
and leave them feeling dirty or confused.

But words can be powerful for good too, Lord.
Words can be used
to make friends,
to show caring,
to make people laugh,
to tell others about you.
Words are powerful, Lord.
Help me use words that bring joy and healing.

Questions about college

I have so many questions about college:
Should I go?
Will it be worthwhile for me?
Will I like it?
Which college should I go to?
Will the work be much harder than in high school?
Can I get good grades there?
Will I find new friends?
Where will the money come from?

Lord, I have so many questions.
Help me find some right answers.
Send me people who can give me good advice.
College is a big step in my life,
and I want it to be a right step.
Guide me to make the right decisions.
Lead me into a good future.

Childhood faith

Lord, when I was younger
believing was so easy.
All the stories in the Bible seemed so real,
and I believed everything.
It was easy then for me to talk about God.

Now things are different.
I have more questions than answers.
My faith is wobbly.
One day I know for sure what I believe,
and another day I'm not sure of anything.
There are so many different ideas.
How can I know which is right?

Help me think through the doubts and questions.
Send me the people and the books I need.
Just as I'm growing in body,
help me grow in understanding and faith.
Let my doubts and questions
be steps
to a stronger and more mature faith.

Tired of school

I'm tired of school, God.
It's all so boring.
There are still weeks before vacation,
and I can't stand doing my work.
I stare at a book for hours, and nothing sinks in.
I can't make my brain work,
and I find so many ways to waste time.

Why do we have to spend so much time in school?
And why do we have to learn so much stuff
that doesn't seem to have any use?
Sometimes I'd like to drop out of school
once and for all.
But I know I need an education
to have the kind of life I want.
I know I *need* an education,
I just wish it weren't so hard to get.

School isn't always this bad.
Sometimes I'm interested in what's going on.
But now I need something
to put life back into learning again.
I'm tired of the same old thing.
Send something fresh and new, Lord.
And, help me hang in there during this dull stretch,
doing as well as I can,
even when I don't feel like it.

I hurt someone

Lord, I hurt someone today.
It's so easy to do.

Sometimes I hurt people accidentally,
when I talk without thinking.
Maybe we start out teasing or fooling around,
but it ends up with someone getting hurt.

Other times I know exactly what I'm doing.
I set out deliberately to hurt someone,
to get even with them.
And sometimes it gives me a feeling of power
to know I can make someone feel bad.

Was the hurt I gave today
accidental or deliberate?
I'm not even sure.
But I am sorry.
Forgive me, Lord.

I know there's enough pain in the world
without my adding to it.
Help me apologize to the person I hurt.
Show me how I can make up for the pain I caused.
Make me more sensitive to the feelings of others.

Why don't you do something?

Lord, there's so much wrong in the world.
Wars all over the place,
with people getting shot and bombed and burned up.
So many hungry people.
So many sick in body or mind.
In lots of countries people have no rights
and very little freedom.
We see all this every day
in newspapers and magazines and on TV.
Why is there so much evil?

Why don't you do something about it, God?
You're supposed to be good and all-powerful.
You could change things.
Why don't you?
Do you need our cooperation?

Help those who suffer everywhere, Lord.
Give them food and freedom,
health and a good life.
Show me what *I* can do
to help make a better world for all people.

First date

There's a girl I like,
and I'm thinking about asking her out.
But I'm afraid.
I know I'll turn red and look stupid.
And what if she says no?
I think she likes me,
but I'm not sure.

If she says yes
I'll be even more scared.
I've never been on a date before,
and I'm not sure how to act
or what to talk about.
I'm afraid—but I'm excited too.
I'm starting a whole new part of my life.

I wonder if she likes me
and if she'll go out with me.
Lord, help me know what to do.

Christmas

In some ways Christmas
doesn't mean as much to me as it used to.
I don't get as excited
about presents and Christmas trees.
Sometimes I feel hollow at this time of year.
I get so busy with shopping and school programs
and church activities and parties
that I don't stop to think about Christmas,
and the meaning of it passes me by.
The birth of a baby 2000 years ago
doesn't seem to have much to do with
my everyday life.
O God, I know the Bible says
that in the birth of this baby
you entered our world in a special way
and became human for us,
for me.

Christmas is a great sign of your love for us,
your willingness to be involved in our lives.
Help me to understand this mystery, Lord,
so that I can celebrate Christmas
with meaning.

Standing up for what is right

Lord, I know some things are right
and some are wrong.
I've been taught this,
and I believe it.
But I don't always know how to stand up
for what I know is right.

Especially when I see kids doing something wrong,
I'm not sure how to act.
Should I tell them they're wrong?
Should I tell adults what they're doing?
Do I have the right to expect others
to live by my ideas of right and wrong?
What is my responsibility?

I don't want people to think I'm too straight,
and I don't want to lose friends.
But I do want to stand up for what's right.
Show me how to do this, Lord.
And give me the courage I need.

I'm depressed

Lord, I'm really feeling down.
Everything seems dull and lifeless.
Nothing seems fun or exciting.
I feel bad all the time,
and I don't know all the reasons why.
Nothing is particularly wrong,
but nothing is right either.
I don't feel good about anything—
school, home, friends, family.
Most of all I don't feel good about myself.

God, you seem so silent and far away.
I wish I could feel that you were here with me
and that you were in control of my life.

Lord, what do I do to get out of this hole?
Help, Lord, I really need you.
Put some joy back into my life.
Help me feel good about something again.
Help me love life again.
Help, Lord.

Jesus died for me

I hear words like "Jesus died for your sins"
or words like "atonement" and "redemption"
and sometimes I can't connect them with my life.
I know Jesus was crucified 2000 years ago,
but I have trouble sometimes
figuring out how that affects me.

Lord, help me understand
Jesus' death and resurrection.
Let it have meaning in my life.
Even when I don't understand it,
help me believe that Jesus died *for me*,
that by his dying and rising
Jesus opened the way to you, O God.

Becoming a man

What does it mean to be a man?
Does it mean being physically strong and tough?
Does it mean being a good athlete?
Or having courage to face dangerous situations?
Or being able to fight and even kill?
Is a man someone who is popular with girls?

What all goes into being a man?
And how do I compare?
What kind of man am I becoming?

Or does being a man mean
becoming more like Jesus?
He was a carpenter with big strong hands.
His friends were rugged fishermen.
He had the strength to drive the money changers
from the temple with a whip.
He had the courage to face a bloodthirsty mob
and withstand mockery and torture.
He had the power to meet death and overcome it.
But he was also gentle
when he took a little child on his lap
or comforted the sick.
He cried when his friend Lazarus died.

How do I compare with this man?
Lord, give me this combination
of tenderness and toughness.
Help me to be both strong and gentle.

Thanks for a good report card

Lord, I feel relieved.
Report cards came out,
and mine was better than I expected.
I'm happy,
and my parents will be happy.

Thanks for helping me understand and remember.
Thanks for good teachers.
Thanks for friends who help me when I need it.

Give me motivation to keep studying
so I'll be prepared for some useful work in life.
Help me keep going over the rough spots
and the times when school is boring.

I don't know yet what I want to be,
but help me while I'm preparing.
Show me how I can best get ready
for a life that is satisfying to me,
pleasing to you,
and helping to others.

I'm restless

God, I'm restless today.
I can't sit still.
I keep jumping from one thing to another.
I can't concentrate on anything.
I don't know what I want to do.

Sometimes I feel like a wound-up spring,
ready to fly apart in all directions.
I have so much energy.
I feel like I could run and run forever.
Lord, thanks for all this energy.
Help me find good ways to release it.

And slow me down, Lord.
You've promised us your peace.
Let me experience some of it now.
Slow me down.
Slow me down.

I love to win

Lord, I love to win.
I want to come in first,
to be on the winning team.
I like to play hard in games and sports.
It's exciting to be faster and more skillful
and to score more points.
Winning feels good,
and losing feels so bad.
When I lose, I get angry at myself or others.
I think people are looking down on me,
and I feel like I'm not worth much.

I like winning,
but I know victory isn't always possible,
in games or in life.
Help me play fair and try hard to win,
and help me accept defeat when I lose.
Help me be a good loser
and a good winner.

My parents are arguing

O God, my parents are arguing again,
and I can't stand it anymore.
They're always fighting over such little things,
trying to prove who's right
and who's to blame.
I feel caught in the middle.
I care about both of them,
and when they fight
I feel like I'm being torn in half.

I wish I could do something to help,
but anything I do seems to make matters worse.
Sometimes I think they might get a divorce,
and then I wonder what would happen to me.
Sometimes when the fighting is really bad,
I think about running away.

Lord, make them stop.
Help them find better ways of getting along.
Help them find ways to work out their problems.
And help me to know what to do.

Forgive us, Lord.
Our family needs you.
Be with us.

Is religion for losers?

Is religion just for losers,
a crutch for people
who are too weak to make it on their own,
a comfort for people
who are homely or uncoordinated or dumb?
Sometimes when I look around church or youth group,
it seems that way.
Many of the people
who are strong and popular and good-looking
aren't there,
but there are plenty of losers.
Some of the weak, mixed-up people
seem to be more interested in religion
than the successful, happy ones.

I know the church is supposed to be
for sinners and weak people,
but is it only for them?
And how do I fit into the picture?
Am I a loser too?
Sometimes I feel that way.

Help me be honest about my weaknesses
and willing to accept others, even the losers.
Help me be aware of my strengths too,
and thankful for them.
Show me how I can use them
to serve you.

Thanks for food

I love to eat!
It seems like I'm hungry all the time.
I love hamburgers and french fries,
malts and ice cream,
spaghetti and pizza,
cake and pie,
and almost everything else that's good to eat.
Thanks, God, for all good food.

While I'm thankful for what I have,
help me remember those who are hungry.
Bless everyone who's fighting against world hunger
by helping people grow better crops,
develop better livestock,
and get their products to market.
Help me find ways I can share my abundance
with those who have less.
May the food I eat strengthen me
to help those who are hungry.

A major mess-up

Lord, I've really messed up my life.
This time it's not some small mistake.
This time it's really bad.
Everybody is mad at me.
No one understands.
I don't understand either.
And I don't know how to repair the damage
or put the pieces back together again.
I need help.

Send someone, Lord.
Help my family and friends to forgive me.
Show me the way out of this confusion.
Help me learn from my mistake.
Bring some good out of this mess.
Help me, Lord.

I can't stand funerals

I can't stand funerals.
I don't like death and dead bodies
and crying people and creepy music.
Everything seems so unnatural.
I feel uncomfortable.
I don't know what to say or how to act.
It's all so strange.

Help me to know what to do and say.
Help me offer some sympathy,
even if it's in fumbling words.
Let me remember that you are stronger than death
and that you are there
with me,
with all the other people.

Those who work in foreign lands

Father, be with everyone who works in foreign lands,
with a strange language and different customs,
away from their family and friends.

Bless missionaries and teachers,
doctors and nurses,
diplomats and soldiers,
technicians and business executives.
Help them bring
knowledge,
hope,
healing,
protection,
and peace.
Be especially with those who are
isolated,
lonely,
or depressed.
Protect those who are in danger,
threatened by violence or disease.

Help us at home
remember them in prayer,
in this way cooperating with you
in their support and care.

The future of the world

Lord, sometimes I really worry
about the future of the world.
I watch TV
and read the papers
and study current events,
and it all makes me wonder.
Will we pollute the earth so much
that human life will be impossible?
Will nuclear war destroy everybody?
Will there be mass starvation
as population zooms out of control?
There are so many problems.
and nobody seems to have the answers.

Help us, Lord.
Help all those who are working for a better future.
all who are helping to feed the hungry,
control pollution,
fight disease,
and establish peace.
Help us keep on trusting that you're in charge
of this world you've created and redeemed.

A good day

It's been a good day.
I didn't do anything stupid.
I didn't get into any fights.
I didn't argue with anybody.
I did all right in school.
Our team won the game.
My friends were good to me.
Our family had a good time together.
Today, everything seemed to go right.
I felt good and laughed a lot.
Thanks, Lord—
thanks for a good day.

Some bad friends

I think I've gotten in with some bad friends.
I like being with them
because they're fun.
They make me laugh,
and they know their way around.

But I know they're not always the best influence on me.
They keep me from studying
or from other work I should do.
When I'm with them,
I say and do things I don't like.

Lord, it's hard to choose good friends.
I felt good when these friends chose me,
and then I didn't see things very clearly for a while.
I know I've made some mistakes.
Help me break from these friends
and find new ones,
some who will be fun to be with
but who will also help me be the kind of person
that I want to be
and that you want me to be.

People in authority

I have trouble with people in authority—
parents, teachers, pastors, leaders.
I feel uncomfortable with them,
unsure of myself.
I always think they're being critical of me.
Sometimes I want to rebel,
to do the opposite of what they want,
to prove my independence.
Or I smart off and talk back to make them mad.
Is this a normal part of growing up?
Or is there something wrong with me?

Lord, forgive me for rebelling.
Give me people in authority that I can trust.
Help me relate to them in good ways.
Show me the right ways to be independent.

She broke up with me

Lord, I don't know what to do.
My girl friend broke up with me,
and I feel rotten.
Now she won't even talk to me.
If she sees me, she turns the other way.
I could understand if she wanted to break up,
but why does she have to avoid me?

I don't get it.
I thought we were good friends.
I thought she liked me.
We seemed to get along so well.
Then this happened.
I wonder what's wrong with me
that made her decide she doesn't like me.
I don't think I've ever felt so bad about anything.

Lord, I still like her,
even if she doesn't like me.
Help me get over the hurt.
Give me some confidence back.
Help, Lord.

Thanks for my family

Lord, thanks for my family.
We're far from perfect—
as you know—
but I really love them
and they love me.
We have our problems and differences and irritations,
but that's only on the surface.
Underneath there's love,
and I'd feel terrible if anything happened to my family.

Lord, keep my family together.
Protect us.
Keep us healthy.
Help us be patient
and care about one another's needs.
Thanks for the good times we have together.

Thanks for this imperfect—
but loving—
family.

"What are you going to do?"

"What are you going to do when you grow up?"
I hate that question.
I get tired of shrugging my shoulders and saying,
"I don't know."
Some kids seem so sure
about what they want to do with their lives.
But I just don't know
what I'd like or what I'd be good at.
One week I think this,
the next week that.
I know I want to do something interesting,
not something boring.
And I want to do something worthwhile,
not something useless.
But there are so many possibilities!

What do you want me to do, Lord?
How do I find out what it is?

Let me know, Lord, what my abilities are
and what work I could do for you
and for other people.
Help me trust that you're leading me
in a sure and quiet way
toward my life's work.

How to witness

I know I'm supposed to witness to others
about Christ and the way of salvation,
but I don't know how.
I feel so unsure of myself.
When I try, I feel embarrassed
and don't know what to say.
I'm afraid people will ask questions I can't answer,
and I have enough questions of my own.

I know I have responsibility for sharing the faith.
Help me know how to do it.
Show me when it's time to speak
and when to keep quiet.
Keep me from being so pushy
that I turn other people off.
Teach me to listen
and to have respect for the ideas of others.
Teach me to know my own faith so I can share.
Give me courage to speak of you
even at the risk of looking foolish.
Teach me to share not only words,
but the love you give us.

I can't stand him

Lord, I'm mad at one of my teachers.
He just isn't fair.
He's not willing to help when we have trouble.
He's sarcastic and tries to embarrass people.
He always gives a big assignment
right before a vacation or a big game.
He plays favorites and has pets.
I can't stand him.

How can I get along with someone like that?
I can't just run away from the situation.
Lord, give me patience to make it through this class
without blowing up.
Show me if there's some way
I can get along better with this difficult person.

I'm grateful that there are some teachers
who are easier to get along with,
who are helpful,
who have a sense of humor,
who care about our feelings.
Thanks for the good teachers, Lord.

Make tomorrow better

O God, it's been a rotten day.
The only good thing about it is that it's over.
Nothing seemed to go right.
I was mad at the world,
and the world seemed mad at me.
Right now I don't like school.
I feel like I don't have any friends.
My family doesn't understand me.
It seems like I'm no good at anything.
I'm not even sure you're there, Lord.
Maybe I'm just talking to myself.

It's been a rotten day.
Forgive this day, Lord.
Wipe it out.
Help me forget it.
Make tomorrow better, Lord.
Make tomorrow better.

I want to be me

I'm tired of being compared with others.
I'm tired of trying
to live up to the performance of people
who are smarter or older
or more gifted or more motivated.
It seems like I always come out second-best.
Why do my parents and teachers
have to compare me with others?
I don't want to be measured by someone else.
I want to be me.

But sometimes it isn't only other people
who do the comparing.
Sometimes I do it to myself.
I look at others and I compare
my grades,
my looks,
my talents,
my performance,
my personality—
and again, I come off second-best.
But I'm tired of feeling inferior.

Lord, help me accept myself
as the unique person you made me.
Help me see that there are
some good things about *me* too.
Let me see what you want to accomplish
in the world, through me.
Help others to accept me
as the person I am.

Thanks for a special friend

Lord, thanks for a special friend
I can really talk to,
someone who's always willing to listen
to my troubles and my ideas
without thinking I'm stupid.
I need a friend like that.
I know I can talk to you about anything,
but sometimes I need a human friend too,
someone like me
who will listen and understand.

I'm glad I have a special friend.
Help me be a good friend too.

Can you hear me?

I have lots of questions about prayer.
When I was small I used to recite prayers
at mealtime and at bedtime.
But now I'd like to make prayer
a part of my whole life.
I don't know how to do that.

Sometimes prayer feels real to me.
But sometimes I feel awkward trying to pray,
and it seems like I'm just talking to myself.
Can you hear me, Lord?
Does it really make any sense for me to pray?
I wonder sometimes if it's just a cop-out.
And I wonder why some prayers go unanswered.

But I know prayer has made a difference
in the lives of other people.
Lord, help me learn how to pray
and help me keep praying.
Help me believe
that you're really there
and that you do hear me.

For the earth

I like to breathe fresh air,
walk in the woods,
swim in clear water,
feel grass under my feet.
I like to see deer in the forests,
hawks in the sky,
salmon in the rivers,
ducks on the lakes.

But sometimes I wonder,
is there any hope for this earth?
I get really angry
when I think about what people are doing:
cutting down forests,
killing wildlife,
polluting the air and the rivers and oceans,
covering everything with concrete and asphalt.

Lord, you've made this world so beautiful,
and we're making it so ugly.
I don't want to live in a dirty, ugly world.
If we keep on polluting it,
people won't be able to live on the earth at all.

God, stop the greedy and careless people
who are destroying the earth.
Help us all love and care for what you've given us.

We're hypocrites, Lord

Lord, we're such hypocrites.
On Sunday when we walk into church,
all dressed up, smiling and pleasant,
people probably think, "What a wonderful family."

But we're a lot different when no one's looking.
As soon as church is over and we get into the car,
the fighting starts.
Mom and Dad start criticizing us,
and we talk back to them
and argue with one another.

And that's what we do too often at home—
criticizing, finding fault, bearing grudges.
Why is it so hard to be a Christian family?
Why is it so hard to love the people close to you?
Why is there such a gap between what we say
and what we do?

Lord, forgive our family
for not being what we should be
and want to be.
Help each person be more patient.
Let all of us do what we can
to make our family life better.
I think we do love one another,
but sometimes we don't show it very well.
We need to know how to get along better.
Teach us, heavenly Father.

Bless the media

Lord, I like radio and TV.
They add music and entertainment to dull hours.
Sometimes when I don't feel like doing anything else,
it feels good to flop in front of the TV set
and watch a good show.
Thanks for sports,
mysteries,
adventures,
comedies,
dramas,
and news.

Bless the people who work in radio and television:
actors, comedians, and musicians,
newscasters, and disc jockeys,
announcers and technicians.
Help them bring us good programs.

Give me good judgment in my use of radio and TV,
so I don't waste my time on worthless shows
or use TV as a substitute for my own living.
Radio and TV are good gifts.
Help me use them wisely.

I did it again

Lord, I did it again.
I promised you I wouldn't,
but I couldn't help myself.

Sometimes I do something I know is wrong.
Then I feel really bad
and promise I won't ever do it again.
And I really mean it.
But a few days later—
or even in a few hours—
I lose my self-control
and I make the same mistake again.

Lord, forgive me
and help me grow in self-control.
But most of all,
keep on forgiving me.

Marriage

Lord, it seems strange,
but sometimes I think about marriage.
It's far away for me,
but I wonder about it anyway.

Sometimes I think I'll stay a bachelor.
I'd be more free that way.
I could do what I want
without having to worry about anyone else.
But other times I think that might be lonely.
Maybe it would be good for me to settle down
with a wife and children.
Then I wonder,
will I be able to find a good wife?
If I find someone I love, will she love me?
How will I know when I find the right person?
So many people seem to marry the wrong person,
and there are so many divorces.
I wouldn't want that.

Lord, I know I don't have to worry about this now,
but sometimes I do anyway.
Help me to trust you,
to believe that you're in charge of my future
and that you'll help me
make a good decision about marriage
when the time comes.

Vacation!

It's vacation!
And I need it!
I thought it would never come.
The last few weeks of school have really dragged by.

But now school's out.
No more classes.
No more assignments.
No more teachers.
No more homework.
Freedom!
Now I can do what I like:
sleep late,
play ball,
hike and camp and fish,
spend time with friends,
or just sit around.

Lord, I need times like this,
time to relax and have fun.
Let this be a good time for me
with friends,
with family,
or by myself.
Thanks for getting me through these past weeks,
and thanks for the freedom of vacation.

Thanks for many things

I know I don't always appreciate
all the good things I have,
and I often take them for granted,
but today I am thankful.
I'm so glad I have
a healthy body,
friends,
my family,
sports and games,
bikes and cars,
parties and fun,
TV and movies and radio,
stereos and bands and choirs,
trees and skies and rivers and lakes,
peace and security.

Lord, you've given me so many good things,
good people,
good experiences.
Help me enjoy them with thankfulness.
Help me to share what I have
and to use these good gifts
for your purposes.